UP CLOSE!

by
Riley Brooks

SCHOLASTIC INC.

© 2013 by Scholastic

ISBN 978-0-545-54126-8

Published by Scholastic Inc.
SCHOLASTIC and associated logos are trademarks and/or registered trademarks of Scholastic Inc.

12 11 10 9 8 7 6 5 4 3 2 1   13 14 15 16 17/0

Printed in the U.S.A.   40
First printing, January 2013

Contents

Introduction

Whether they're lighting up the silver screen in the year's biggest blockbusters, hanging out on your favorite TV shows, or belting out the catchiest songs on the radio, you can always count on your favorite stars to keep you entertained. But have you ever wondered how your favorite actresses made it big? What do your favorite singers do in their spare time? What are today's biggest actors really like behind the scenes? Well, read on to find out all about your fave celebs!

C-400   4   PFRM

Big Time Rush

★ ★ ★ Star Stats: ★ ★ ★

Name: James David Maslow

Birthday: July 16, 1990

Hometown: New York City, New York

Siblings: older brother, Philip, and half sister, Ali

Pet: dog named Fox

Favorite Food: Italian

Favorite Book: *Ender's Game* by Orson Scott Card

Hobbies: surfing, horseback riding, practicing Saito Ninjutsu (a form of martial arts)

Name: Kendall Francis Schmidt

Birthday: November 2, 1990

Hometown: Wichita, Kansas

Siblings: older brothers Kenneth and Kevin

Pets: an adorable pig

Favorite Food: pizza

Favorite Book: *Fahrenheit 451* by Ray Bradbury

Hobbies: rock climbing, surfing, skateboarding

★ ★ Star Stats: ★ ★

Name: Carlos Roberto Pena, Jr.

Birthday: August 15, 1989

Hometown: Columbia, Missouri

Siblings: brothers Antonio, Javi, and Andres

Pets: dogs Stella and Sydney

Favorite Food: spaghetti

Favorite Book: the Harry Potter series

Hobbies: writing music, scuba diving

Name: Logan Phillip Henderson

Birthday: September 14, 1989

Hometown: Temple, Texas

Siblings: sister, Presley

Favorite Food: pizza

Favorite Book: *Norwegian Wood* by Haruki Murakami

Hobbies: wakeboarding, skateboarding, snowboarding, watching sports

Big Time Rush is both an awesome boy band
and one of the highest-rated TV shows on
Nickelodeon. The show centers around four best
friends from Minnesota who form a boy band.
The band members are James Maslow as "James
Diamond," Logan Henderson as "Logan Mitchell,"

Kendall Schmidt as "Kendall Knight," and Carlos Pena, Jr. as "Carlos Garcia." More than 1,500 people auditioned for the show, so the guys had some stiff competition! The show's creator wrote each part based on the actor playing it, which means that each of the guys is a lot like his character.

In addition to filming the show and a few made-for-TV *Big Time Rush* movies, the guys also have a record deal with Columbia and have released two albums: *BTR* in October 2010 and *Elevate* in November 2011. Their biggest singles have been "Love Me Love Me," "You're Not Alone," and "Superstar." Big Time Rush has toured a lot and the band One Direction and singer Rachel Crow have both opened for them.

Big Time Rush is working on their third album, *Windows Down,* which they plan to release in 2013. Fans can't wait!

Victoria Justice

✦ ★ ★ Star Stats: ★ ✦ ★

Name: Victoria Dawn Justice

Birthday: February 19, 1993

Hometown: Hollywood, Florida

Parents: bio dad Mark Justice, mom Serene Reed, and step-dad Mark Reed

Siblings: younger sister, Madison

Pets: dog, Sophie

Favorite Food: steak with a loaded baked potato

Favorite Color: turquoise

Favorite Romantic Movies: *Sleepless in Seattle* and *When Harry Met Sally*

Hobbies: karaoke, reading, swimming

Triple threat Victoria Justice was born in Hollywood, Florida, and started modeling and acting in commercials at age eight. At age eleven, she was accepted to a performing arts school in Hollywood, California, and she moved across the country to go to school there.

Living in Los Angeles gave Victoria more chances to audition for acting roles. She guest starred on *The Suite Life of Zack and Cody* and in several independent films before she got her big break on the Nickelodeon show *Zoey 101*. When *Zoey 101* ended, Nick offered Victoria her own show. *Victorious* is about teens at a performing arts high school. Victoria stars as "Tori Vega," a reluctant performer with a big voice, and she loves getting the chance to act, sing, and dance all on one show!

During breaks in filming *Victorious*, Victoria has filmed several made-for-TV movies including *Spectacular!*, *The Boy Who Cried Werewolf*, and *Fun Size*, and guest starred on a ton of Nick shows. She's also been busy writing and recording songs for her first album, which came out in late 2012.

Rachel Crow

★ ★ ★ Star Stats: ★ ★ ★

Name: **Rachel Crow**

Birthday: **February 19, 1993**

Hometown: **Mead, Colorado**

Parents: **Barbara and Kelly Crow**

Siblings: **younger sister, Hannah**

Pets: **a Maltese-Yorkie puppy named Charlie**

Favorite Food: **Chinese food and chocolate**

Favorite Books: **the Diary of a Wimpy Kid series and the Dork Diaries series**

Favorite Movie: *Titanic*

Hobbies: **doodling, swimming, going to the movies**

When Rachel Crow auditioned for national TV talent show *The X Factor*, the bubbly thirteen year old was the youngest contestant on the show, but she made it all the way to the top five before being eliminated. Though she didn't win, she still signed a record deal with

Columbia records and a TV development deal with Nickelodeon after the contest, so things are turning out just fine for this rising star!

Nickelodeon created a new show just for Rachel. It's going to be a comedy with plenty of awesome music. But before her show begins, Rachel got the chance to guest star on other popular Nick shows like *Figure It Out*, *Big Time Rush*, and *Fred*.

Rachel released her first EP (a mini album) titled *Rachel Crow* in July 2012. Rachel helped write some of the songs on the album, including the anti-bullying anthem "Mean Girls," which has been a hit with fans around the world. She spent most of 2012 on tour with Big Time Rush performing and meeting with fans, and is currently hard at work on her first full-length album. Rachel's career has just begun and fans can't wait to see what she does next!

Andrew Garfield

✦ ★ Star Stats: ★

Name:
Andrew Russell Garfield

Birthday:
August 20, 1983

Hometown:
Los Angeles, California

Parents:
Lynn and Richard Garfield

Siblings:
older brother, Ben

Pet:
a dog

Hobbies:
surfing, swimming, traveling

Super-cute Andrew Garfield was born in California, but grew up in England. He got into acting as a teenager with a local theater group starring in plays. When he was sixteen, he moved on to television with starring roles in several British television shows. After a couple of years, Andrew made the leap to the big screen. But Andrew's big break was starring opposite Jesse Eisenburg in *The Social Network*, the hit film about the founders of Facebook.

After making a splash in the film world, Andrew took a break to star in his first Broadway play: *Death of a Salesman*. He even won a Tony Award for his performance! His next role was as the superhero Spider-Man in *The Amazing Spider-Man* with Emma Stone. Comic fans loved Andrew as the geeky Peter Parker and his alter ego Spider-Man, and he looked great in the spider suit!

Fans are eager to see what Andrew's up to next, and chances are, this talented star won't disappoint them!

Jennifer Lawrence

Name: Jennifer Shrader Lawrence

Birthday: August 15, 1990

Hometown: Louisville, Kentucky

Parents: Karen and Gary Lawrence

Siblings: older brothers Ben and Blaine

Pet: a dog

Favorite Food: peanut-butter-and-jelly sandwiches

Favorite Color: purple

Favorite Books: *The Other Boleyn Girl* by Phillipa Gregory; *Raise High the Roof Beams, Carpenters* by J.D. Salinger; *The Rum Diary* by Hunter S. Thompson

Hobbies: horseback riding, playing basketball, field hockey, softball

Jennifer Lawrence started acting when she was sixteen with a starring role on *The Bill Engvall Show*. After that, Jennifer appeared on numerous television shows and in several independent films before landing the starring role in an independent drama that won her an

Academy Award nomination for Best Actress. Since then, Jennifer has starred in bigger blockbusters like *X-Men: First Class* and *The Hunger Games*.

Jennifer played "Katniss Everdeen" in The Hunger Games, the film adaptation of the *New York Times* bestselling book series. It was a big role, and Jennifer trained in archery, rock climbing, combat, and parkour to prepare for the part. She even dyed her hair brown! There are three more films in the series, and Jennifer is already filming the sequel, *Catching Fire*. She has also recently wrapped four other movies. With a packed filming schedule, multiple award nominations, and interest from numerous Hollywood directors, the odds are in favor of Jennifer Lawrence having a long and successful career.

Josh Hutcherson

★ ★ ★ Star Stats: ★ ★ ★

Name: Joshua Ryan Hutcherson

Birthday: October 12, 1992

Hometown: Union, Kentucky

Parents: Michelle and Chris Hutcherson

Siblings: younger brother, Connor

Pets: dogs Driver, Diesel, and Nixon

Favorite Food: pizza

Favorite Movies: *Fight Club*, *The Lion King*

Favorite Book: *The Catcher in the Rye* by J.D. Salinger

Hobbies: watching sports, cooking

When you think of Josh Hutcherson, you probably think of "Peeta" in *The Hunger Games,* but this Kentucky cutie has been acting for a long time!

Josh landed his first role when he was nine years old and has been working ever since.

Josh has appeared in many films, including *The Polar Express; Kicking & Screaming; Howl's Moving Castle; Little Manhattan; Zathura; RV; Bridge to Terabithia;* and *Journey 2: The Mysterious Island.* Critics always give him rave reviews and Josh has won a number of awards for his performances. Josh loves taking roles in different genres and considers himself lucky to have worked with a lot of fantastic actors in his career.

Landing the part of "Peeta Mellark," the baker's son and second tribute from District 12, in *The Hunger Games* was really exciting for Josh. He loved working with Jennifer Lawrence and filming all of the awesome action sequences in the film. He'll be playing "Peeta" in the next three films, and he can't wait for fans to see them!

Zachary Gordon

★ ★ ★ Star Stats: ★ ★ ★

Name: Zachary Adam Gordon

Birthday: February 15, 1998

Hometown: Oak Park, California

Parents: Linda and Ken Gordon

Siblings: older brothers Josh and Kyle

Favorite Food: hot dogs and chicken fingers

Favorite Books: *The Candy Shop War* by Brandon Mull and *Diary of a Wimpy Kid* by Jeff Kinney

Hobbies: video games, playing basketball, watching basketball

Zachary Gordon has been acting since he was eight years old. Zach's first few roles were guest parts on TV shows including *How I Met Your Mother, All of Us, Because I Said So, Desperate Housewives, MADtv, 24,* and *iCarly*. With his expressive voice, Zachary has also done a ton of voiceover work on shows like *Robot Chicken; The Mighty B!; Handy Manny; Special Agent Oso; Batman: The Brave and the Bold;* and *Ni Hao, Kai-lan.*

Next, Zach moved on to film roles in *Georgia Rule; National Treasure: Book of Secrets; Four Christmases; Beverly Hills Chihuahua 2; Ted;* and *R.L. Stine's The Haunting Hour.* But the role Zach is most well known for is starring as "Greg Heffley" in *Diary of a Wimpy Kid; Diary of a Wimpy Kid: Roderick Rules;* and *Diary of a Wimpy Kid: Dog Days* based on the popular book series. Zachary was already a fan of the books, so it was easy to get into character. He loves playing "Greg" and is hoping for many more *Diary of a Wimpy Kid* movies in the future!

Chloë Moretz

★ ★ ★ Star Stats: ★ ★ ★

Name: Chloë Grace Moretz

Birthday: February 10, 1997

Hometown: Atlanta, Georgia

Parents: McCoy Lee and Terry Moretz

Siblings: older brothers Brandon, Ethan, Colin, and Trevor

Pets: dogs Missy, Fuller, Jaxon, & Bella

Favorite Food: pasta

Favorite Color: green, pink, and blue

Favorite Movies: *Breakfast at Tiffany's* and *Gone With the Wind*

Hobbies: playing video games, going to concerts and movies, traveling, swimming, playing with her dogs

Chloë Grace Moretz is a Southern girl making a big splash in the acting world. At only sixteen years old, she already has a very impressive resume. Chloë landed her first big part when she was only six years old, and she won a Young Artist Award for her performance. She's had dozens of television and film roles since then, and she recently appeared in *Diary of a Wimpy Kid*, a film based on the popular children's book series. She then starred along with Asa Butterfield in *Hugo*, a film based on the *New York Times* bestselling children's book *The Invention of Hugo Cabret*, and she is slated to star as "Emily" in *Emily the Strange*, an upcoming film based on the popular comic.

Impressive acting skills and resume aside, Chloë also has quite an eye for fashion. Whether she's running errands in favorite teen brands like Urban Outfitters and American Apparel or rocking haute couture looks on the red carpet, Chloë has become a fashion icon. This rising star clearly has a long, exciting career ahead of her.

Lily Collins

★ ★ ★ *Star Stats:* ★ ★ ★

Name: Lily Jane Collins

Birthday: March 18, 1989

Hometown: Guildford, Surrey, England

Parents: Phil Collins and Jill Tavelman

Siblings: half sister, Joely, and half brothers Nicholas, Matthew, and Simon

Favorite Designers: Marc Jacobs, Dolce & Gabbana, Vivienne Westwood

Favorite Color: teal

Favorite Books: the Harry Potter series, the Mortal Instruments series, the Hunger Games trilogy

Hobbies: traveling, shopping, writing

Lily Collins was born to be a star. Her dad is rock star Phil Collins, so Lily grew up around the entertainment industry. As a teen, Lily wrote for *Elle Girl, Seventeen, Teen Vogue,* and the *Los Angeles Times* and went on to study broadcast journalism at the University of Southern California.

In 2008, Nickelodeon signed Lily up as a correspondent who interviewed celebs. Lily soon found herself going on auditions and appearing in a few episodes of *90210* and in the movies *The Blind Side* with Sandra Bullock and *Priest* with Paul Bettany. In 2011, Lily co-starred with cutie Taylor Lautner in *Abduction*, and then starred as "Snow White" in a comedy with Julia Roberts called *Mirror Mirror*.

Her next role will be as "Clary Fray" in the film adaptation of the *New York Times* bestselling young adult series The Mortal Instruments. She's so dedicated to the role she's set up a Twitter feed for her character!

Having a famous dad helped her break into the industry, but these days Lily's star power is bright enough to get her any role she wants!

Cody Simpson

★ ★ ★ Star Stats: ★ ★ ★

Name: Cody Robert Simpson

Birthday: January 11, 1997

Hometown: Gold Coast, Queensland, Australia

Parents: Brad and Angie Simpson

Siblings: younger brother, Tom, and younger sister, Alli

Pets: a Shih Tzu named Zoey

Favorite Food: Italian food, ice cream

Favorite Color: blue and green

Favorite Book: *Ice Station* by Matthew Reilly

Favorite Movie: *Iron Man*

Hobbies: swimming, singing, surfing, playing guitar, skateboarding

Cody Simpson is an Australian pop singer whose soulful voice and surfer-boy good looks have made him a hit in the U.S. Cody got his start recording YouTube videos in his bedroom in Australia in 2009. Just a year later, Cody was discovered and signed to a U.S. record deal with Atlantic Records.

Cody released his first single "iYiYi" featuring Flo Rida and followed that up with "Summertime" a few months later. His EP *4 U* came out at the end of 2010 and fans absolutely loved it. In between touring and performances, Cody has released two more EPs: *Coast to Coast* and *Preview to Paradise*.

Cody has been hard at work writing and recording songs for a full-length album. He would love to branch out as an actor someday, but right now he's focused on his music. He can't wait to get his first full album out and perform for all his fans on his own tour!

Bella Thorne

★ ★ ★ Star Stats: ★ ★ ★

Name: Annabella Avery "Bella" Thorne

Birthday: October 8, 1997

Hometown: Pembroke Pines, Florida

Parents: Reinaldo and Tamara Thorne

Siblings: older brother, Remy, and older sisters Dani and Kaili

Pets: a dog named Krystal, six cats, and a turtle

Favorite Food: chocolate

Favorite Books: *Wuthering Heights* by Emily Bronte

Favorite Movies: *Beauty and the Beast*, *Brave*, and *The Little Mermaid*

Hobbies: working with animals, dancing, painting, bowling

Bella Thorne is the youngest of four talented kids. She began modeling alongside her older siblings when she was only six months old and started acting when she was just six.

In 2006, the entire Thorne family moved to Hollywood so that Bella could have more opportunities to act. Sadly, Bella's dad died in a car accident just a year later. Bella was devastated, but she pushed on with her acting, knowing how proud her dad would have been of her. She starred in two spooky movies—*The Seer* and *Forget Me Not*—and won a role alongside cutie Taylor Lautner on the short-lived TV show *My Own Worst Enemy*.

Soon after, Bella landed the role of "CeCe Jones" on the Disney show *Shake It Up* alongside Zendaya Coleman. In 2012 Zendaya and Bella also starred together in the made-for-TV movie *Frenemies*. Next up for the pair is a *Shake It Up* movie.

With Bella's talent and gorgeous looks, she's sure to be a Hollywood star for a long time to come!

Zendaya Coleman

☆☆☆ Star Stats: ☆☆

Name: Zendaya Coleman

Birthday: September 1, 1996

Hometown: Oakland, California

Parents: Claire and Kazembe Coleman

Siblings: older sister, Zendoria

Pets: a Giant Schnauzer named Midnight

Favorite Food: spaghetti

Favorite Color: pink

Hobbies: singing, dancing, designing clothes

Zendaya Coleman grew up in the theatre—literally! Her mom was the house manager for the California Shakespeare Theater and Zendaya helped out often. As she got older, she performed in lots of plays and even joined the theatre's student conservatory program. She also modeled and did several commercials before landing her current role on Disney Channel's hit show *Shake It Up* as "Requelle 'Rocky' Blue," an aspiring dancer on a music TV show.

Bubbly Zendaya is currently working on a *Shake It Up* movie. In addition to her acting skills, Zendaya has a phenomenal voice. She signed a record deal with Hollywood Records and has released several singles including "Swag It Out," "Dig Down Deeper," and "Fashion is My Kryptonite." She plans to record and release her first album over the next year and she would also love to design her own fashion line.

With acting, singing, and fashion on her plate, Zendaya is just taking things one day at a time. She knows she has plenty of time to accomplish all of her dreams!

Justin Bieber

★ ★ ★ Star Stats: ★ ★ ★

Name: Justin Drew Bieber

Birthday: March 1, 1994

Hometown: Ontario, Canada

Current Town:
Los Angeles, California

Siblings: half sister, Jazmyn, and half brother, Jaxon

Pets: a dog named Sam

Favorite Food: spaghetti and meatballs, tacos

Favorite Movies: the Rocky Series

Hobbies: hockey, pulling pranks, making funny videos

Justin Bieber was just a normal Canadian boy when he entered a local singing contest at the age of twelve. His mom videotaped the performance and uploaded it to YouTube so far-away family members could see it. The video got so many hits that Justin began recording and posting clips of himself singing other songs. Before he knew it, he had a huge fan base and was getting calls from record labels.

Justin signed with manager Scooter Braun and with Island Def Jam Records, where Usher became his mentor. Since then Justin has released several albums, including *My World, My World 2.0, Under the Mistletoe,* and *Believe.* He has sold a total of more than 15 million albums! Justin's biggest singles include "One Less Lonely Girl," "One Time," "Baby," "Somebody to Love," and "Boyfriend." Girls everywhere fell in love when they saw Justin's adorable smile and heard his super-catchy music!

Justin is focusing most of his energy on his music and tours, but he has found a little bit of time for some fun projects, including a behind-the-scenes movie about his life called *Never Say Never.* Justin also loves to make funny videos and takes the opportunity to hang out with friends and family whenever he has a little downtime. What a sweetie!

Selena Marie Gomez

★ ★ ★ Star Stats: ★ ★ ★

Name: Selena Marie Gomez

Birthday: July 22, 1992

Hometown: Grand Prairie, Texas

Parents: mom Mandy Teefy and step-dad Brian Teefy, bio dad Ricardo Gomez

Pets: rescue dogs Baylor, Willie, Wallace, Fina, Chip, and Chazz

Favorite Food: homemade Rice Krispies treats, dill pickles

Favorite Book: *Dear John* by Nicholas Sparks

Favorite Movies: *The Wizard of Oz*

Hobbies: painting and drawing, singing, surfing, skateboarding, basketball

Selena Gomez started acting on the long-running children's show *Barney & Friends* when she was seven years old. But her big break came during a Disney open-call audition in 2004. Disney loved Selena and moved her to Hollywood immediately. Once there, she guest starred on *The Suite Life of Zach and Cody* and *Hannah Montana* before her own show, *Wizards of Waverly Place*, premiered.

With her TV career taking off, Selena was also able to pursue movies and music. She has starred in a number of films including *Another Cinderella Story*, *Princess Protection Program*, *Ramona and Beezus*, *Monte Carlo*, *Hotel Transylvania*, and *Spring Breakers*. She's currently working on the movies *Thirteen Reasons Why*, *Hot Mess*, *The Getaway*, and *Aftershock*.

As the lead singer for the band Selena Gomez and the Scene, Selena has also released three albums, which have sold over 2.3 million copies worldwide. On top of all that, Selena has her own clothing line, volunteers for several charities, and still makes time for her friends and family. Amazing!

Taylor Swift

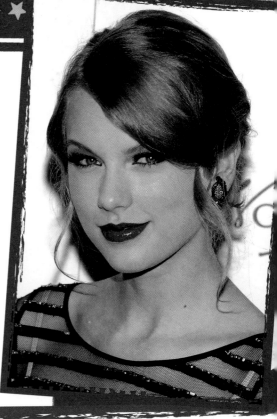

★ ★ ★ Star Stats: ★ ★ ★

Name: Taylor Alison Swift

Birthday: December 13, 1989

Hometown:
Wyomissing, Pennsylvania

Parents: Scott and Andrea Swift

Siblings: younger brother, Austin

Pets: a cat named Meredith

Favorite TV Show:
Grey's Anatomy

Favorite Food: cheesecake

Favorite Color: white

Hobbies: songwriting, boating,
watching movies

Taylor Swift is the reigning queen of country music. She's already released three multi-platinum albums: *Taylor Swift, Fearless,* and *Speak Now,* and has toured all over the world. Taylor's fourth album, *Red,* went on sale at the end of 2012, and her fans were thrilled! Taylor has sold more than 22 million albums and has won numerous awards for her singing and songwriting including six Grammy Awards, ten American Music Awards, six Academy of Country Music Awards, and seven Country Music Association Awards.

Taylor writes or helps write every song on her albums, and she draws inspiration from just about every aspect of her life. She has been romantically linked to stars like Taylor Lautner, Joe Jonas, John Mayer, Cory Monteith, and Jake Gyllenhaal—and she's written songs about all of them!

Taylor has also dabbled in acting. She's guest starred several times on *CSI: Crime Scene Investigation* and has had small roles in big feature films, including *The Lorax*, an animated film based on the Dr. Seuss children's book. Taylor has been on the lookout for more film roles, but she's holding out for the perfect parts for her!

Taylor really is the whole package. She writes, sings, acts, and has become a force in the fashion world. At almost six feet tall with a slim frame, Taylor is every designer's dream model. She loves to play with fashion and has been featured as a cover model on dozens of magazines—including *Vogue*.

Taylor has no plans to slow down. She's constantly writing, releasing new singles, touring, and taking on new projects. With the support of her fans, her reign as queen of country music is sure to be a long one!

One Direction

★ ★ ★ Star Stats: ★ ★ ★

Name: Harry Edward Styles

Nickname: Barry

Birthday: February 1, 1994

Hometown: Holmes Chapel, England

Siblings: older sister, Gemma

Favorite Bands: Foster the People, Coldplay, Kings of Leon, The Beatles

Likes: Laser Quest

Dislikes: roller coasters, olives

Name: Liam James Payne

Nickname: Ian

Birthday: August 29, 1993

Hometown: Wolverhampton, England

Siblings: two older sisters, Ruth & Nicola

Favorite Bands: Two Door Cinema Club, Bing Crosby, John Mayer

Likes: surprises, aftershave, singing in the shower, his pink hair straightener

Dislikes: flying, spoons

★ ★ ★ Star Stats: ★ ★ ★

Name: Zain Javadd Malik

Nickname: Wayne, Zayn

Birthday: January 12, 1993

Hometown: Bradford, England

Siblings: sisters Doniya, Waliyha, and Safaa

Favorite Bands: Usher, Robin Thicke, Michael Jackson

Likes: scary movies, dancing, tattoos

Dislikes: crust on sandwiches

Name: Louis William Tomlinson

Nickname: Hughy

Birthday: December 24, 1991

Hometown: Doncaster, England

Siblings: sisters Charlotte, Félicité, Daisy, and Phoebe

Favorite Bands: Bombay Bicycle Club, The Fray

Likes: sunbathing, silly voices, practical jokes

Dislikes: not being able to Tweet on planes

Name: Niall James Horan

Nickname: Kyle

Birthday: September 13, 1993

Hometown: Mullingar, Ireland

Siblings: older brother, Greg

Favorite Bands: The Script, Ed Sheeran, Bon Jovi

Likes: soccer, the color yellow

Dislikes: mayonnaise, clowns

One Direction got their start on the seventh season of the famous United Kingdom TV singing competition *The X Factor*. Liam Payne, Harry Styles, Niall Horan, Louis Tomlinson, and Zayn Malik each auditioned separately, but became a group after their auditions. Sadly, One Direction finished in third place, but they were offered a record deal with Syco Music and recorded their first album right after the show.

One Direction made history on March 13, 2012 when they released their album *Up All Night* at number one on the American charts. They were the first British group to ever have a number one debut in the U.S. It was already a big hit with fans in the UK and Europe, and the guys were glad that American fans loved the album just as much.

The guys toured the U.S. with Big Time Rush on a leg of their "Better With U" Tour, and made guest appearances on several TV shows including Nickelodeon's *iCarly*, *The Today Show*, and *Saturday Night Live*.

1D has reached superstardom, but they aren't planning to slow down anytime soon. The boys have already won several awards, including three Teen Choice Awards and a Brit Award! The group's second album hit stores in September 2012 and they've announced a world tour that will keep them on the road for all of 2013. One Direction has lots of other opportunities, too. They have a development deal in place with Nickelodeon for a TV show and have partnered with some cool brands like Pokémon and Nokia. One thing is certain: No matter what the future holds, it's looking very bright for the cuties of One Direction!

Willow & Jaden Smith

★ ★ Star Stats: ★ ★

Name: Willow Camille Reign Smith

Birthday: October 31, 2000

Hometown: Los Angeles, California

Parents: Will Smith & Jada Pinkett Smith

Siblings: older brother, Jaden & older half brother, Trey

Pets: a bulldog named Little Homie

Favorite Food: macaroni & cheese

Favorite Color: purple

Favorite Book: *My Favorite Color Is…* by E. Moore

Hobbies: shopping, hanging out with friends, listening to music, baking

Name: Jaden Christopher Smith

Birthday: July 8, 1998

Hometown: Malibu, California

Parents: Will Smith & Jada Pinkett Smith

Siblings: younger sister, Willow & older, half brother Trey

Pets: a bulldog named Little Homie

Favorite Food: pancakes

Favorite Book: *Fledgling Jason Steed* by Mark A. Cooper

Hobbies: practicing Wushu (a form of Chinese martial arts)

Willow Smith is a super-sassy singer and actress and the daughter of superstars Will Smith and Jada Pinkett Smith. Willow first came on the scene in the 2007 movie *I Am Legend*. She followed that with *Kit Kittredge: An American Girl* and *Madagascar: Escape 2 Africa*.

Willow is also very passionate about music, so she took a break from acting in 2010 to record her first album on Jay-Z's record label Roc Nation. Her very first single "Whip My Hair" went platinum and hit number 11 on the Billboard Hot 100 chart.

Up next, Willow is slated to star in a remake of *Little Orphan Annie* with new music produced by Jay-Z. She's also been hard at work on her first album, *Knees and Elbows*. And she's serving as an ambassador for Project Zambia— a charity that helps African kids suffering from AIDS—with big brother Jaden. What a superstar!

Jaden Smith is Willow's big brother, and he's every bit as talented as his little sis! He started acting with guest roles on the television shows *All of Us* and *The Suite Life of Zack and Cody*. His big-screen debut came in 2006 in *The Pursuit of Happyness*. Jaden won a 2007 MTV Movie Award for his emotional performance.

In 2008 Jaden had a small role in *The Day the Earth Stood Still*, a sci-fi drama. Jaden's next project was starring in 2010's *The Karate Kid* with Jackie Chan. Jaden did a lot of training to prep for the role and was able to do a lot of his own stunts. He filmed two movies in 2012—*Amulet* and *After Earth*. He's super-proud of both films and can't wait for fans to see them.

A love of music runs in the Smith family, and Jaden released two singles in 2012. With his talent and work ethic, chances are he'll be as big of a star as his dad someday!